My Claws Are Huge and Black

by Joyce Markovics

Consultant:
Christopher Kuhar, PhD
Executive Director
Cleveland Metroparks Zoo
Cleveland, Ohio

BEARPORT
PUBLISHING

New York, New York

Credits

Cover, © Robert Marien/Corbis; 4–5, © Kuznetsov Alexey/Shutterstock;
6–7, © Alexey Kuznetsov/Dreamstime; 8–9, © wisawa222/Shutterstock;
10–11, © kurt_G/Shutterstock; 12–13, © ZSSD/Minden Pictures/Corbis;
14–15, © Davemhuntphotography/Dreamstime; 16–17, © Robert Marien/Corbis;
18–19, © Lamyai/Shutterstock; 20–21, © Lamyai/Shutterstock; 22, © sanpom/
Deposit Photos; 23, © blackeagleEMJ/Shutterstock; 24, © Eric Isselee/Shutterstock.

Publisher: Kenn Goin
Senior Editor: Joyce Tavolacci
Creative Director: Spencer Brinker
Design: Debrah Kaiser

Library of Congress Cataloging-in-Publication Data in process at time of publication (2017)
Library of Congress Control Number: 2016006802
ISBN-13: 978-1-944102-60-9 (library binding)

For more information, write to Bearport Publishing Company, Inc., 45 West 21st Street, Suite 3B,
New York, New York 10010. Printed in the United States of America.

10 9 8 7 6 5 4 3 2 1

Contents

What Am I?

Look at my tail.

It is curved and pointy at the tip.

5

I have eight
short legs.

My body is hard, shiny, and black.

8

9

I have
many eyes.

They are tiny
and round.

I carry my babies
on my back.

12

They are
yellowish white.

Fine hairs cover
my body.

15

My claws are
huge and black.

17

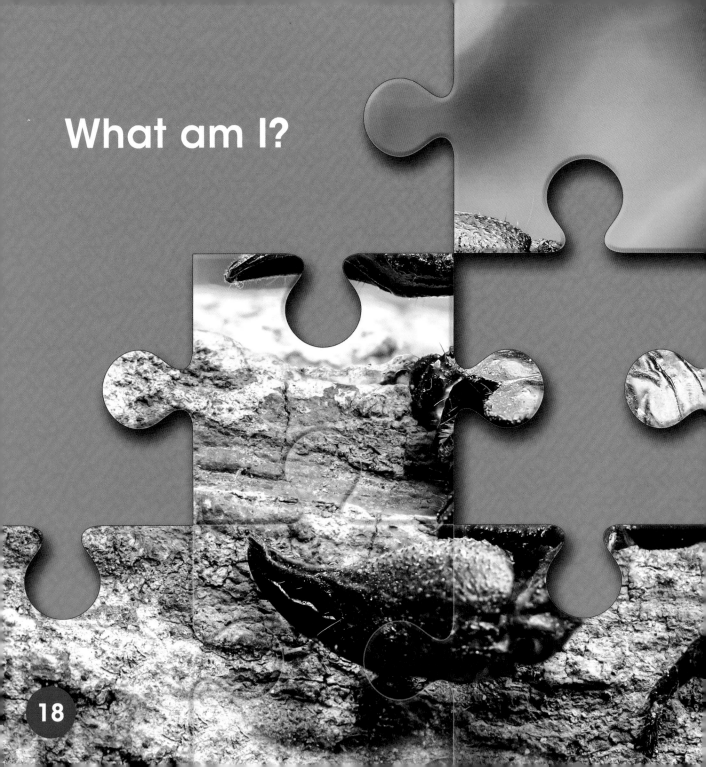

What am I?

Let's find out!

I am an emperor scorpion!

Animal Facts

Emperor scorpions are related to spiders. They grab and crush their food with huge claws called pincers. Scorpions also have venom in their tails and can sting other animals.

More Emperor Scorpion Facts

Food:	Mice, insects, and other small animals
Size:	6.5 inches (16.5 cm), including the tail
Weight:	About 1.1 ounces (31 g)
Life Span:	5 to 8 years
Cool Fact:	Emperor scorpions do not have to drink water. They get all the water they need from the food they eat!

Adult Emperor Scorpion Size

Where Do I Live?

Emperor scorpions live in hot, wet forests in Africa.

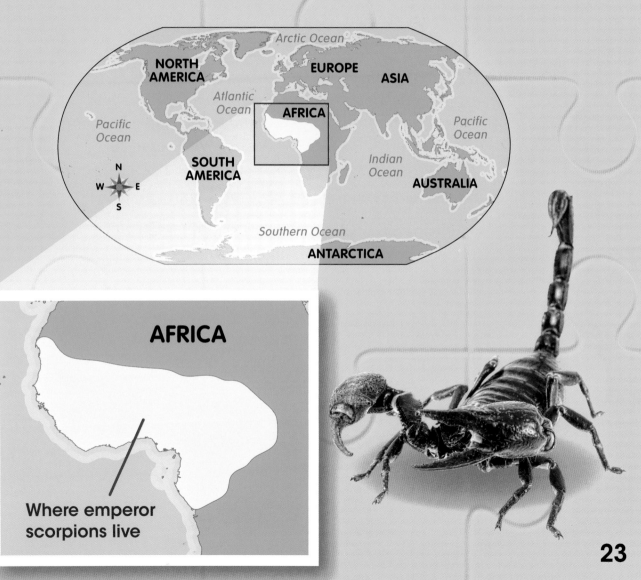

Where emperor scorpions live

Index

Read More

Lunis, Natalie. *Stinging Scorpions (No Backbone! The World of Invertebrates).* New York: Bearport (2009).

Pringle, Laurence. *Scorpions! (Strange and Wonderful).* Honesdale, PA: Boyds Mills Press (2002).

Learn More Online

To learn more about emperor scorpions, visit **www.bearportpublishing.com/ZooClues**

About the Author

Joyce Markovics lives in a very old house in Ossining, New York. She has a soft spot for creatures with hard exoskeletons.